Tasha Tudor's Favorite Christmas Carols

Tasha Tudor's Favorite Christmas Carols

Illustrated by Tasha Tudor and Linda Allen

DAVID McKAY COMPANY, INC.
New York

Illustrations by Tasha Tudor, Courtesy of
American Artists Group, Inc.

Design by Jane Preston

Library of Congress Cataloging in Publication Data
Main entry under title:

Tasha Tudor's Favorite Christmas carols.

1. Carols. 2. Christmas music. I. Tudor,
Tasha. II. Title: Favorite Christmas carols.
M2065.T23 [(M5400)]   783.6'55'2   77-29242
ISBN 0-679-20975-1

10 9 8 7 6 5 4 3 2 1

Manufactured in the United States of America

Contents

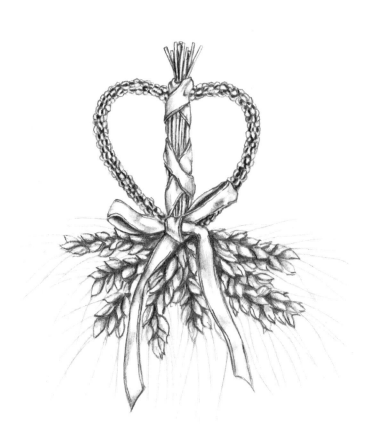

Preface

An old chapbook, published in England in the early 1500s, describes a carol as a "song of joyful character, associated with good cheer as an element in Christmas and other seasonal observations."

The word carol stems from the French *carole*, meaning a dance in which people sing the refrain of a song while they stamp around in a circle. French carols, or *Nöels*, are among the oldest. They were written, for the most part, anonymously, composed by clerics and teachers during the early Middle Ages. The songs soon traveled to England and other parts of Europe, where they were popularized by wandering minstrels, pageantries, and church festivals.

Saint Francis of Assisi is credited with bringing carols into formal church worship. On Christmas Eve, 1223, he re-created the setting of the first Christmas Eve with some borrowed farm animals and a statue of the Christ Child. Francis composed and sang carol-like songs to accompany his tableau.

The oldest printed source for the words of early carols was discovered in a commonplace book written by a London grocer between 1500 and 1536. But most carols were handed down orally, from generation to generation, before they were finally recorded by folk-song collectors.

The carols that are included in this book are among the oldest, the best loved, and the most familiar. They are easily played on sight by the amateur pianist, and in addition, simple guitar chords for the songs are included at the end of the book.

—Tasha Tudor

Hark! The Herald Angels Sing

Hark! The Herald Angles Sing

Charles Wesley, the composer of more than 4000 published hymns and cofounder of Methodism, wrote the original stanzas of "Hark! The Herald Angels Sing." Over a century later, William Cummings slightly rearranged Wesley's words and set them to a chorus from a Felix Mendelssohn cantata.

Hark! The Herald Angels Sing

Charles Wesley (1707–1788)

Felix Mendelssohn (1809–1847)

Hark! the herald angels sing, "Glory to the new-born King; Peace on earth, and
Christ, by highest heaven a - dored; Christ, the e - ver-last - ing Lord, Long desired be-

mer-cy mild, God and sinners rec-on-ciled!" Joyful, all ye nations, rise,
hold Him come, Fix in us Thy humble home. Veiled in flesh the Godhead see,

Join the triumph of the skies; With an - gel - ic hosts proclaim, "Christ is born in
Hail th'Incarnate De - i - ty, Pleased as man with man to dwell, Je - sus our Im-

Beth-le-hem!"
man - u - el.
} Hark! the herald angels sing, "Glo - ry to the newborn King."

The First Nowell

Traditional English

Unknown

The first No-well the angels did say, was to certain poor
They look-ed up and saw a star shining in the

shepherds in fields as they lay; In fields where they lay keeping their
east, be-yond them far, And to the earth it gave great

sheep, On a cold winter's night that was so deep. No-well, No-
light, And so it con-tinued both day and night.

well, No-well, No-well, Born is the King — of Is-ra-el.

The First Nowell

"The First Nowell" is one of the oldest ballad carols, popular for more than two centuries. The earliest known printed version appeared in 1833, but the song is believed to be at least three hundred years older. Although its name has often been misspelled "Nöel," its source has never been traced to France. Many musicologists believe that the carol may have originated in Cornwall, England.

O Come, All Ye Faithful

O Come, All Ye Faithful

The Latin hymn *"Adeste Fideles"* dates from the mid-eighteenth century. Most historians believe than an English music copyist and Latin teacher, John Francis Wade, wrote the words and set them to music in Douay, France, between 1740 and 1745. The well-known English words, "O Come, All Ye Faithful," were translated from the Latin and first appeared in print in *Murray's Hymnal*, published in London in 1852.

O Come, All Ye Faithful

John Francis Wade (1712–1786)

(?)John Francis Wade

O come all ye faith-ful, joy-ful and tri-umphant, O come ye, O
Sing, choirs of an-gels, sing in ex-ul-ta-tion, O sing, all ye

come ye to Beth - le - hem; Come and be - hold Him, born the King of an-gels;
cit-i-zens of heav'n a-bove! Glo - ry to God, all glo-ry in the high-est!

Refrain

O come, let us a-dore Him, O come, let us a-dore Him, O come, let us a-

dore Him, — Christ, — the Lord!

9

Angels We Have Heard on High

Traditional French

Unknown

An - gels we have heard on high, Sweetly singing o'er the plains,
Shepherds, why this ju - bi - lee? Why your rapturous strain prolong?
Come to Beth - le - hem and see Him whose birth the an - gels sing;

And the mountains in re - ply, Ech - o - ing their joy - ous strains.
What the glad - some tid - ings be Which in - spire your heav'nly song?
Come, a - dore on bend - ed knee Christ the Lord, the new - born King.

Glo - - - - - - - - - - - - - - - ri - a

in ex - cel - sis De - - - - - - - o.

Angels We Have Heard on High

The composer of "Angels We Have Heard on High" is unknown. Musicologists have traced the origin of its melody to an old carol, *"Les Anges dans Nos Campagnes,"* which they believe was written by a French composer during the eighteenth century.

Away in a Manger

Away in a Manger

When "Away in a Manger" appeared in *Dainty Songs for Little Lads and Lasses*, published in the United States in 1887, the book's compiler wrote that the carol had been composed in Germany by Martin Luther. But several decades later, a member of the Library of Congress discovered that the carol had first appeared in a book published in 1885 by the Evangelical Lutheran Church of North America. The words and music of the carol had been written by an American composer, William James Kirkland.

Away in a Manger

William James Kirkland (1847?–?)

William James Kirkland

A - way in a manger, no crib for His bed, The lit - tle Lord
The cat - tle are lowing, the Ba - by a-wakes, But lit - tle Lord

Je - sus laid down His sweet head. The stars in the sky looked
Je - sus, no cry - ing He makes. I love Thee, Lord Je - sus; look

down where He lay, The lit - tle Lord Je - sus, a - sleep on the hay.
down from the sky, And stay by my cradle till morning is nigh.

While Shepherds Watched Their Flocks

Nahum Tate (1652–1715)

Arr. by George Frideric Händel (1685–1759)

While   shep - herds   watched their   flocks   by   night,   All
"Fear   not,"   he   said — for   might - y   dread   Had
"To   you,   in   Da - vid's   town,   this   day,   Is

seat - ed   on   the   ground,   The   an - gel of the   Lord   came down,
seized their troubled   mind   "Glad ti - dings of great joy   I   bring,
born of   Da - vid's   line,   The   Sav - iour, who is Christ the Lord,

And   glo - ry shone a - round,   And   glo - ry shone a - round.
To   you and all man - kind,   To   you   and all   man - kind.
And   this shall be the   sign,   And   this   shall be the   sign."

While Shepherds Watched Their Flocks

In 1708, "While Shepherds Watched Their Flocks by Night" was the only Christmas carol sanctioned by the Church of England for use in worship services. Nahum Tate, who was Poet Laureate of England at the time, transcribed the verses from *Luke* 2: 8–15. Although the verses have been sung to several different tunes, the most familiar melody for the carol in America is an adaptation of an aria from *Siroë of Persia*, an opera first produced by Handel in London in 1728.

O Little Town of Bethlehem

Phillips Brooks (1835–1893)   Lewis H. Redner (1831–1908)

O lit - tle town of Bethle - hem, How still we see thee lie!
For Christ is born of Ma - ry, And gathered all a - bove,

A - bove thy deep and dreamless sleep The si - lent stars go by;
While mortals sleep, the an - gels keep Their watch of wond'ring love.

Yet in thy dark streets shin - eth The ev - er - last - ing Light;
O morning stars, to - geth - er Pro - claim the ho - ly birth,

The hopes and fears of all the years Are met in thee to - night.
And prais - es sing to God the King, And peace to men on earth!

19

O Little Town of Bethlehem

On Christmas Eve, 1865, the eloquent American preacher, Phillips Brooks, made a trip on horseback from Jerusalem to Bethlehem. Three years later, back in Philadelphia, his memory of seeing the Holy Land village for the first time prompted him to write the words of "O Little Town of Bethlehem" for the children of his congregation. The author's verses were set to music by his church organist, Lewis H. Redner, who said that the melody had come to him as a "gift from heaven" in a dream.

Silent Night

Joseph Mohr (1792–1848)   Franz Xavier Grüber (1787–1863)

Si - lent night,   ho - ly night! All is calm,   all   is bright,
Si - lent night,   ho - ly night! Dark-ness flies, all   is light,

Round yon Vir - gin   Moth-er and Child   Ho - ly In-fant, so   ten-der and mild,
Shep-herds hear the   an - gels   sing,   "Al - le - lu - ia! hail to the King

Sleep in heaven-ly   peace,   Sleep in heaven-ly   peace.
Christ the Saviour is   born!   Christ the Saviour is   born!"

23

Silent Night

When the organ in an Austrian village church broke down on Christmas Eve, 1818, the assistant pastor, Joseph Mohr, decided to rectify the mishap. He gave a poem he had written to the church organist, Franz Grüber, and asked him to set it to music arranged for two soloists, a chorus, and guitar accompaniment. That same evening the well loved song, "Silent Night," was heard for the first time. Shortly after Christmas, the organ repairman gave a copy of the carol to a troupe of Tyrolean singers, who popularized the song wherever they went. Since they never mentioned the composer's name, Franz Joseph Haydn's brother, Michael, was given credit for the music, possibly because of his published arrangement of the melody. But in 1854, a special investigating committee discovered the truth about the composition.

Deck the Halls

Deck the Halls

The Welsh have always had the reputation of being a musical people, and many carols are of Welsh origin. Although "Deck the Halls" is one of the most lively and familiar of all Welsh carols, very little is known about its history. Mozart used the melody in a violin and piano duet, which he composed during the early eighteenth century.

Deck the Halls

Traditional Welsh

Unknown

Deck the halls with boughs of hol - ly,
See the blazing yule be - fore us,
Fast a-way the old year pass-es,
Fa, la, la, la, la, la, la, la, la.

'Tis the sea-son to be jol-ly,
Strike the harp and join the cho-rus,
Hail the new, ye lads and lass-es,
Fa, la, la, la, la, la, la, la, la.

Don we now our gay ap - par - el,
Fol - low me in mer - ry measure,
Sing we joy-ous all to-geth-er,
Fa, la, la, la, la, la, la, la, la.

Troll the an-cient Christ-mas car - ol,
While I tell of Christ-mas treasure,
Heed-less of the wind and weather,
Fa, la, la, la, la, la, la, la, la.

It Came upon a Midnight Clear

Edmund H. Sears (1810–1876)

Richard S. Willis (1819–1960)

It came up-on a mid-night clear, That glo-rious song of old,
Still through the clo-ven skies they come, With peace-ful wings un-furled,

From an-gels bend-ing near the earth, To touch their harps of gold;
And still their heavenly mu-sic floats O'er all the wea-ry world;

"Peace on the earth, good will to men, From heav'n's all-gra-cious King."
A-bove its sad and low-ly plains They bend on hov'ring wing,

The world in sol-emn still-ness lay, To hear the an-gels sing.
And ev-er o'er its Ba-bel sounds The bless-ed an-gels sing.

29

It Came Upon a Midnight Clear

Edmund H. Sears, the author of "It Came upon a Midnight Clear," was a Harvard Divinity School graduate. The song's composer, Richard S. Willis, graduated from Yale and later became a music critic for the New York *Tribune*. When the verses first appeared in the *Christian Register* in 1850, the clergyman–editor of the publication wrote: "I always feel that, however poor my Christmas sermon may be, the reading and singing of this hymn are enough to make up for all deficiencies."

We Three Kings of Orient Are

John H. Hopkins, Jr. (1820–1891)   John H. Hopkins, Jr.

We three kings of O - ri - ent are; Bearing gifts we traverse a-far,
Born a King on Bethle-hem's plain, Gold I bring to crown Him a-gain,
Frankin-cense to of-fer have I, In-cense owns a De - i - ty nigh;
Myrrh is mine, its bit-ter per-fume Breathes a life of gathering gloom:

Field and fountain, moor and mountain, Following yon - der star.
King for ev - er, ceas - ing nev - er, O - ver us all to reign.
Prayer and praising all men rais-ing, Worship Him, God on high.
Sorrowing, sigh - ing, bleed-ing, dy - ing, Sealed in the stone-cold tomb.

Refrain after each verse:

O star of won-der, star of night, Star with roy - al beau-ty bright,

Westward leading, still pro-ceed-ing, Guide us to Thy per-fect light.

31

We Three Kings of Orient Are

"We Three Kings of Orient Are" is a relatively modern composition in the true carol tradition, and one of the few American carols to achieve international popularity. Both words and music were written around 1857 by Dr. John H. Hopkins, Jr., while he was serving as Rector of Christ Church in Williamsport, Pennsylvania.

Joy to the World!

Isaac Watts (1674–1748)

Unknown

Joy to the World!

Although the music for "Joy to the World!" has often been mistakenly attributed to Handel, no one knows for certain who wrote the original melody that inspired Isaac Watts to write the lyrics for this famous tune. Watts published the verses in 1719 in *Psalms of David Imitated in the Language of the New Testament*, an adaptation of the 98th Psalm, which includes the line, "Make a joyful noise unto the Lord, all the earth."

O Holy Night

O Holy Night

Translated by John S. Dwight (1826–1881)

Adolphe Charles Adam (1803–1856)

O ho - ly night! The stars are brightly shin - ing, It is the
Led by the light of Faith se-rene-ly beam - ing, with glowing

night of the dear Saviour's birth, Long lay the world in sin and error
hearts by His cra-dle we stand; So, led by light of a star sweetly

pin - ing, 'Till He appeared, and the soul felt the worth. A
gleaming, Here came the Wise Men from the O - rient land. The

thrill of hope the wea - ry world rejoi - ces, For yon - der breaks a
King of kings lay thus in low - ly manger, In all our tri - als

new and glorious morn! Fall on your knees! ————— O
born to be our Friend; He knows our need, ————— He

hear ————— the an-gel voi - ces! O night ————— di-
guards ————— us all from dan - ger, Be - hold ————— your

vine! ————————— O night ——— when Christ was born! O
King! ————————— Be - fore ——— the Low-ly bend! Be-

night ————————— di - vine! ————— O night, O night di - vine!
hold ————— your King! ————— Be - fore the Low-ly bend!

O Holy Night

Ever since "O Holy Night" was written over a century ago, it has been the most popular of all Christmas solo songs. Adolphe Charles Adam, the French composer of more than fifty stage works, including the ballet *Giselle*, wrote the hymn in Paris during the first half of the nineteenth century. The verses were translated into English in 1852 by an American music journalist, John Dwight.

O Christmas Tree

O Christmas Tree

In the sixteenth century, lighted evergreens became part of the Christmas decorations and observations of most European countries. Approximately two centuries later, during the Revolutionary War, Hessian soldiers introduced the lighted fir tree to America. Although the composer of "O Christmas Tree ("*O Tannenbaum*") is unknown, the song's origin has been traced to Germany, where it remains the favorite of all carols.

O Christmas Tree
(O Tannenbaum)

Traditional German

Unknown

O Christmas Tree, O Christmas Tree, Thy leaves are green for - ev - er. O
O Christmas Tree, O Christmas Tree, A flame with lights and splendor. O

Christmas Tree, O Christmas Tree, A symbol for the faith - ful. They
Christmas Tree, O Christmas Tree, Thy

all are green in summer's prime, They all are green at Christmas time. O
boughs shine forth with candles' glow, And flash on ea - ger eyes be -low. O

Christmas Tree, O Christmas Tree, Thy leaves are green for - ev - er.
Christmas Tree, O Christmas Tree, A symbol for the faith-ful.

What Child Is This?

William Chatterton Dix (1837–1898)   Old English Folk Song "Greensleeves"

What Child is this, who, laid to rest, On Mary's lap is sleeping? Whom
Why lies He in such mean e - state, where ox and ass are feeding? Good

an - gels greet with anthems sweet, While shepherds watch are keep - ing?
Christians, fear: for sin - ners here The si - lent Word is plead - ing:

This, this — is Christ the King, Whom shepherds guard and an - gels sing:
Nails, spear, shall pierce Him through, The cross be borne, for me, for you:

This, this — is Christ the King, The Babe — the Son — of Ma - ry.
This, this — is Christ the King, The Babe — the Son — of Ma - ry.

What Child Is This?

The words of "What Child Is This?" were written in the late 1880s by William Chatterton Dix, an English hymn writer and insurance company manager. The verses are sung to the melody of "Greensleeves," one of the most famous of all English folk songs. When a license for printing the music was issued to Richard Jones in 1580, the composition was called, "A New Northern Dittye of the Lady Greene Sleeves." Shakespeare later used the song in several of his plays, including *The Merry Wives of Windsor*.

Good King Wenceslas

Good King Wenceslas

"Good King Wenceslas" was originally a spring carol, "*Tempus ad est Floridium*." In the mid-nineteenth century, John Mason Neale, an English clergyman and historian, composed an entirely new set of verses, based on an old Bohemian legend about a benevolent tenth-century ruler. The part of the king is often sung by one voice, the part of the page by another, and the narrator's voice by a chorus.

Good King Wenceslas

John Mason Neale (1818–1866)   Unknown

God Rest You, Merry Gentlemen

Traditional English

Unknown

God rest you, merry gen - tle - men, Let nothing you dis - may, Re-
From God our Heav'nly Fa - ther A bless-ed An-gel came; And
Now to the Lord sing prai - ses, All you with - in this place, And

member Christ our Sav - iour Was born on Christmas Day, To save us all from
un - to cer-tain shep-herds Brought tidings of the same: How that in Bethle-
with true love and brotherhood Each other now em-brace; This ho-ly tide of

Chorus

Sa-tan's pow'r When we were gone a-stray;
hem was born The Son of God by name. } O — ti - dings of com - fort and
Christ - mas All other doth de-face. }

joy, comfort and joy, O — ti - dings of com-fort and joy.

God Rest You, Merry Gentlemen

The composer of "God Rest You, Merry Gentlemen" is unknown. In *A Christmas Carol*, Charles Dickens described how irate Scrooge became upon hearing the opening bars of this traditional English carol. Scrooge, busy in his counting house, was regaled by a caroler. "At the first sound of 'God rest you merry gentlemen, let nothing you dismay,' Scrooge seized the ruler with such energy that the singer fled in terror."

Guitar Chords